INSTINCT OF A WARRIOR

THE COURAGE TO CREATE

INSTINCT OF A WARRIOR

THE COURAGE TO CREATE

Balraj Goel

Worldwide Published by

Pendown Press

PENDOWN PRESS LLP
An ISO 9001 & ISO 14001 Certified Co.,
Regd. Office: 3767A, Kanhaiya Nagar,
Tri Nagar, Delhi-110035
Ph.: 8130886000, 9650072927
E-mail: info@pendownpress.com
Branch Office: 1A/2A, 20, Hari Sadan, Ansari Road,
Daryaganj, New Delhi-110002
Ph.: 011-45794768
Website: PendownPress.com

Edition: 2025
Price: ₹ 299
ISBN: 978-93-6338-022-8

Layout and Cover Designed by Pendown Graphics Team
Printed and Bound in India by Thomson Press India Ltd.

॥ मंगल भवन, अमंगल हारी,
द्रबहु सु दसरथ, अजिर बिहारी ॥

This book is dedicated to everyone who has been a part of my journey. Your inspiration, unwavering support, and guidance have shaped my path and strengthened my resolve. This is just a small part of the journey made possible by your good wishes, and I carry your encouragement with me every step of the way.

Table of Contents

Foreword

This book is not just a story—it's a journey about building a successful business and a meaningful life. It's about my father, a man who turned his hard work, positive attitude, and strong values into a thriving business. His life shows that success isn't just about making money; it's about building relationships, facing challenges, and living with purpose.

My father is not an engineer by degree, yet he led an engineering company with his "never give up" spirit. His story is proof that anyone can achieve great things with determination and belief in themselves. His journey is a beacon of hope for those who feel they don't have the "right cards" in life.

This book is a collection of simple lessons, values, and ideas that guided his journey. In today's world, where material things often take over, it's a reminder that real success comes from the love we share, the problems we solve, and the impact we leave on others.

One thing my father always says is, "Do good, and good will come to you." This book carries that message for everyone. It's written to inspire you to stay strong, dream big, and always lead with kindness and honesty.

And if nothing else, this book will make you smile, because life has a funny way of teaching us that even when things seem tough, a little humor and a lot of determination can take you far.

As my father would say, "If you can't fix the problem, at least fix your attitude—and then watch how everything else starts to fall into place."

Rohit Goel

Acknowledgements

My parents, Mr. Som Prakash Goel and Mrs. Shakuntala Devi, are my greatest role models. Their unwavering love, guidance, and values have brought me to where I am today. I am truly grateful for everything they have done.

To my wife, who has stood by me in every situation. You have handled all family responsibilities with great skill and dedication. Thank you from the bottom of my heart.

To my children, Rohit Goel and Pooja Goel, and my grandchildren, Anshul, Sayesha, and Taksh, who are the source of my happiness and inspiration. Sending you lots of love!

To my brothers, Bharat Raj Goel, Dev Raj Goel, Vinod Goel, and Shiv Goel, who guided and supported my decisions.

To my team at Reva, who have been like partners, mentors, and family. Thank you for walking this journey with me.

To our customers, who have shared their experiences and knowledge with us during this journey—thank you for trusting us and being our inspiration.

To my friend, Mr. Dinesh Verma, CEO of Pendown Press, and his team, who supported us throughout this creative process and provided great suggestions.

To the universe for giving me the ideas and strength to complete this book. I am grateful for the love, support, and guidance at every step.

And finally, to all my loved ones who have been with me on this journey—thank you for your unwavering support, encouragement, and affection. Even if your names are not mentioned, you always hold a special place in my heart.

Without the support of all of you, it would not have been possible for me to move forward with confidence.

Thank You!

Bal Raj Goel

Preface

After more than 56 years in the industry, I have learned that success isn't just about the work we do but the values that guide us along the way. Over the years, I've had the privilege of facing challenges, learning from them, and growing both personally and professionally. This book is a reflection of that journey, a journey shaped by hard work, dedication, and a constant desire to improve. That's why, in this book, I've highlighted the key aspects that guided me to success, and I believe these insights will help you in your journey as well.

Through this book, I want to share with you the experiences, lessons, and moments that have shaped my career and my outlook on business and life. I believe that no matter where you start, with the right attitude and perseverance, you can overcome any obstacle and achieve your goals.

I am grateful to everyone who has been part of my journey, whether as a colleague, a friend, or a mentor. This book is as much yours as it is mine. My hope is that it helps you navigate your own path and inspires you to keep moving forward, no matter the challenges that come your way.

This book is for anyone ready to explore new paths to success. I hope it proves to be inspiring for you.

Thank you for taking the time to read this. I hope you find something in these pages that resonates with your own experiences.

CHAPTER 1

Introduction to My Younger Self

My childhood was very different from the way kids grow up today. It wasn't just about me and my siblings; it was a whole big group, a joint family. Imagine a house full of 12-15 kids living together, and during vacations, that number would shoot up to more than 20! It was like living in a mini village inside our own home. We didn't have any fancy gadgets, but we had something far more valuable—teamwork and unity.

You see, the way work was divided back then was simple and natural. If one lady started giving us kids a bath, she would make sure all of us took turns in a proper line. One lady took care of cooking, another managed cleaning, and so on. Everything happened smoothly without anyone telling us what to do—it just worked. I even heard stories about women nursing babies, not because they were the real mother, but because it was all about helping one another.

I was born and raised in Delhi, but my heart always had a special place for my village, Naya Shahar, where my grandmother lived. That village was a world of its own—simple, peaceful, and full of harmony. In fact, we were so lucky that our neighbors would often bring us fresh milk, sometimes even more than we needed. In fact, even today, I make sure to take my family to my village whenever I get a chance. Whenever we're on our way to Chandigarh or traveling somewhere nearby, I always make a stop there, at our home.

As for me, I was a pretty naughty kid, always getting into trouble. I remember one time at my mama ji's house when we were having lunch with kadhi. My youngest mama went to the kitchen to bring the kadhi which was very hot. Just as he was about to sit down, I pulled his chair, and you can guess what happened next—mama ji fell down quite hard and the kadhi spilled all over him! he had some hot kadi on him, and I, of course, ran out of the house faster than a cheetah. My mama ran after me, but thankfully, my elder mami stopped him. That was my kind of trouble!

There was always a relationship of love and respect with Bhabhi Ji (my elder brothers wife). I remember one incident when a golgappa vendor came near our house on the street. The vendor was being called by someone ahead, but neither Bhabhi Ji nor I let him go. We ended up eating all the golgappas ourselves, finishing the entire cart!

My grandfather used to run a sewing machine and fan agency at Devnagar, Karol Bagh while my grandmother lived in the village, mostly alone. During summer vacations, my younger brother, sister, and I would stay with her for about a month. Those days were full of simple pleasures. My grandmother would make the most delicious roti, spread ghee on it, and serve it with salt and spices. Even today, I sometimes crave that roti. The funny part is, when I am sick and the doctors tell me not to eat spicy or salty food, I still go ahead and eat that same roti with ghee and spices—and it makes me feel better every time!

One of my favorite memories was of the summer vacations when we would visit the mango fields. We had a few mango trees, and as kids, we would climb up and pluck the ripest mangoes, bringing them home to enjoy. I remember one time when I was up in the tree, throwing mangoes down. One of my cousins went to pick one up and suddenly ran back shouting that there was a big snake nearby. I was frozen in fear! I spent the next hour up in that tree, trembling with fear, while my cousin went to get help from the villagers. Eventually, they came and helped me down.

All in all, my childhood was full of fun, mischief, and love. Of course, there were some pressures—like schoolwork and studies—but those days taught me valuable lessons about unity, teamwork, and the simple joys of life. These lessons are something I carry with me even today.

Not being a good student, I entered business by default. Being an average student, I was able to think and act like 99.8% of people in the country. I accepted this fact and believed that whatever your gut says should be pursued—and pursued with determination. Remaining positive all the time is crucial because it keeps alive the belief that you might be able to achieve what you want. Of course, failures come too, but they are not the end. My father, who was a government officer, used to say, "Your bread and butter is safe, and you have a place to sleep in so why not work hard and take risks to build a business?

❍ ❍ ❍ ❍

CHAPTER 2

A Passion for Machines

As I mentioned before, my grandfather owned a shop that dealt in Usha Sewing Machines and various other items. After my grandfather's death, I used to sit at the shop and help repair sewing machines and fans whenever the mechanic was not around. My college was just across the street from his shop, with a small empty space in between. It was this very space that inspired me to start something new—a workshop for car repairs. Though I was enrolled in college, my heart was always with machines, and I found it hard to sit through lectures when I could be getting my hands dirty with something I truly loved.

Even back then, I had this immense curiosity about fixing things—taking them apart and putting them back together. So, I spent more time in that shop than in my classes, learning the ropes of car repairs. But as you can imagine, this led to a problem. My attendance in college started to drop significantly, and it became clear that I might not meet the attendance requirements to sit for exams.

But like I always say, where there's a will, there's a way. One day, our commerce professor, Mr. Matha, came to the car workshop and asked for a mechanic to start his car parked in the college ground. I accompanied him. There was a small problem in the carburetor which I fixed and started the car. He was impressed by my skills and wanted to pay me for my work. However, true to my nature, I refused to take any money. Instead, I made a humble request: "I'm a student in your class, but I don't attend regularly. Would you help me out by marking my attendance so I can sit for the exams?" I asked for what I truly needed at that time. He helped with attendance not only with his subject but with others too.

In reality, the only class I actually attended was English at 8:30 AM, which lasted until 9:15 AM. After that, I would rush straight to my shop, open it by 9:30 AM, and stay there for the rest of the day. It wasn't about skipping college; it was about pursuing my passion for machines and learning from real-world experience.

In the end, this was more than just a clever solution to a problem. It was a lesson in resourcefulness, in doing what you love with integrity, and in finding ways to make things work—no matter the obstacles. This approach to life, driven by determination and passion, became the foundation for everything I later achieved.

From Marriage to Milestones

In November 1974, Sunita and I met for the first time, marking the beginning of our journey together. I was passionate and hardworking. At that time, she was staying with her brother, Dr. Jindal. Every weekend, I would visit her, bringing a bouquet of flowers. At that time, I earned ₹400 and used to tell her, "We'll have to manage with just this." She was such a great and understanding lady.

I am especially thankful to her, as she has been cooperating with me through everything to this very day. Her support allowed me to concentrate fully on my work, without the burden of worrying about home, children, or their studies. Sunita took care of everything with the best we could afford. I can't remember a single incident where Sunita said something that created tension in my mind. I firmly believe that God has been guiding me, helping me meet people who have supported and guided me in achieving my targets.

In September 1977, during a flight to Jaipur, the plane was hijacked. I was sitting on the first seat, 1-D. We were in the aircraft for almost 14 hours. I used to smoke at that time and asked one of the hijackers if I could step outside for a cigarette. Surprisingly, he allowed it, as he had taken 2-3 cigarettes from me earlier. I told him I would request someone on the runway for a cigarette and bring back some for him too. When I got down, the police approached me and asked for details about the number of hijackers, their locations, and their weapons. This information might have helped them plan our release.

However, the scariest moment came when one of the hijackers placed a hand grenade in my lap while lighting his cigarette. It was truly a terrifying experience. I was very scared, but I never lost courage. Rohit was just 1.5 years old at the time, and when we finally returned to Delhi, I became highly emotional. Our photos appeared in almost every newspaper across the country.

After that, whenever we had any trips planned, Sunita would tell me that we should not travel by plane, especially considering what happened during that incident. But I always reassured her, as I am a big devotee of Hanuman Ji, and I know he is always with me and will always protect me from any such situation.

I am fortunate to have had the unwavering support of my family. My son, Rohit, is exceptionally hardworking and employs modern techniques to achieve business heights I never dreamed of.

I am a Rotarian and have actively participated in many philanthropic activities. I have also contributed to Sai Dham, and other social causes from time to time.

In 1983-84, we received a major order from BHEL Trichy for manual handling systems. From there, we never looked back. Slowly, we transitioned from manual to electrical equipment, growing our turnover from ₹27,000 to ₹60 crore today. This growth came from meeting skilled people, learning from them, and developing equipment in line with world-class practices. It was a combination of factors: design, material knowledge, manufacturing processes, quality procedures, customer interaction, marketing, and—most importantly—after-sales service.

We have always considered ourselves to be the customer's representative. Most of the improvements in our products have come from listening to our customers' feedback. I traveled 15 to 20 days a month for sales and marketing. It was often our technological edge that helped us secure deals.

Slowly and steadily, with Rohit taking charge, we grew from manufacturing 100-ton equipment to 250-ton equipment. This brings immense satisfaction and a sense of achievement.

Another important aspect of my work is how I treat my employees. I see them as part of my family. Their welfare has always been my first priority, even above customer satisfaction. For me, there has never been a distinction between senior and junior employees—they are all equal and essential to our success.

My Advice

My advice to anyone is to pursue your dreams and follow your gut. Your sincerity and honesty are the ultimate deciders of your destiny. Believe in the mantra: *"Jahan chaah hai, vahin raah hai"* (Where there's a will, there's a way), and pursue your dreams with relentless effort.

Looking back, every challenge taught me something, and every success strengthened my journey. Now, let me take you along as I share my business story in detail—how we struggled, faced challenges head-on, and built a path for myself and my family. This is my journey of resilience and determination..

CHAPTER 3

Reva's Values Run Deep

Roots of Hard Work and Dedication

My grandfather, Lala Pyare Lal Ji, was the first and most educated person in our family, even at a time when education was rare, and not many people valued it. During that period, when education was scarce, he stood out as a shining example of learning. He was a matriculate of his time and had a good command of both written and spoken English and Urdu. In those days, most government work was conducted either in Urdu or English. My grandfather worked as an 'Arjiniwas,' a petition writer. He would sit under a tree in Kharar Tehsil, where he would write petitions for villagers and others, often accepting a small fee, which was sometimes in the form of barter—such as a simple sweet box. He was always ready to help his community, serving them in his own way, and showing his commitment to his values of humility and service.

He strongly believed in the power of education and wanted to give his children the best opportunities possible. My father, under my grandfather's guidance, attended D.A.V. College in Lahore, where he completed his B.A. in Economics (Hons.) with excellent results. He ranked probably second or third in Lahore University, a clear reflection of the dedication and hard work that was ingrained in him from an early age. My mother used to say that my father would often proofread for some of the most respected publishers in Delhi after office hours. Though it made him work late, this helped support the large family of five brothers and two sisters. His extra efforts ensured that the family was well taken care of and laid the foundation for the values of perseverance and commitment that he passed down.

To further his career, my father took the Senior Accounts Services (S.A.S.) exams while working as a stenographer with the Ministry of Finance. His commitment to his studies was remarkable—he would even keep his feet in water to stay awake and study longer. His hard work paid off when he passed the S.A.S. exam and was promoted to the position of an accountant. His career continued to grow, and he was transferred to the A.G.C.R., where he became an Accounting Officer. In the early 1960s, he was sent to Tees Hazari, Delhi, as a treasury officer, a role that involved much public interaction. His honesty and integrity made him well-liked by everyone who came in contact with him.

While working for the government, my father's entrepreneurial spirit also began to shine. In the early 1960s, he opened a printing press, which later was managed by our Fufa Ji. He didn't stop there—he also started a dry cleaning shop and a small workshop that initially focused on assembling sewing machines. With very little investment, this small workshop slowly grew into a manufacturing unit producing spare parts for tractors and other machines. His ability to see opportunities and work hard to make them successful was a key part of his character.

After completing his studies at Hindu College, my brother took over the workshop and moved it to Rohtak Road to expand it further. His hard work and determination began to pay off, and in 1966, we became a supplier of Escorts. Over time, we grew into TURNER BROTHERS, and our business expanded significantly. We started producing 23 items for Escorts Tractors, 32 items for Rajdoot Motorcycles, 58 items for Eicher Tractors, and 24 items for the Vehicle Factory in Jabalpur, along with 15 items for Punjab Tractors. This growth was the result of years of hard work, determination, and a deep-rooted belief in quality and service, principles that were passed down through generations.

Guided by Greatness

Our parents always taught us to respect elders and love the younger ones. This lesson has been the foundation of my deep respect for my elder brother. Whatever he said, I obeyed without question—even if it meant standing in the sun for 10 hours, I would do it without a second thought. He has always been more than a brother to me; he is my guru. Even today, I continue to learn from him about manufacturing, and his guidance still helps me in many ways.

Hard work, dedication, and love for others have been the guiding principles that we, as brothers and sisters, learned from our father, Shri S.P. Goel. Being in a government job, he was not restricted to the usual 9-to-5 schedule. He was an exceptionally hardworking individual who set up many ventures, ultimately handing them over to relatives because he wanted everyone to settle well in life. Among these ventures were the Reva Sewing Machine Agency, a dry-cleaning unit and a Printing Press.

His love for people was so profound that even after 24 years of his passing, his friends' children still respect us. Dr. Raj Aunty often talks about my father's greatness and how he helped in building their house.

He used to say that the dharma of a baniya is to "serve society with employment and do charity through your business."

His friendly nature greatly helped us in acquiring the Okhla factory, securing loans, and thereby building Reva into a strong and stable establishment.

❍ ❍ ❍ ❍

CHAPTER 4

Core Values: The Pillars of My Life

Lessons That Built My Foundation

As discussed in the last chapter, the values my parents taught me have been the foundation of everything I've done in life. They were extremely hardworking and always believed in doing the right thing, no matter how difficult it seemed. They used to say,

दो रोटी कम खा लेना, लेकिन कभी किसी का गलत मत करना।

These values didn't just shape me—they've also been passed down to my children. It's with their blessings that we've been able to reach where we are today.

One value that stands out for me is the importance of focusing fully on whatever you are doing. If you're playing, then focus only on playing. If you're studying, give it your full attention. And this applies to business too—when you're working, don't let your mind wander. Stay fully present in the moment. This habit of giving my complete focus to each task has helped me tremendously in life and business.

Taking Risks

I'll share one story that I still remember vividly. One morning, while having tea and reading the newspaper, I saw an ad for a tender. I had no clue about the details, but I turned to my wife, Sunita, and asked, "Should I go for it?" She encouraged me, and I decided to take a chance. I submitted the tender, and to my surprise, it got allotted. That moment taught me a big lesson—sometimes, you just have to gather courage and take the leap. Once the tender was approved, we worked hard to complete the project successfully, and from there, things started falling into place. Slowly but surely, I began to see the results of my efforts.

This experience taught me that having a vision is essential, but equally important is the willingness to take risks and turn opportunities into success.

Leading with Integrity and Unity

Leadership isn't just about running a business; it's about how your values shape your actions and relationships. For me, one of the most important values in business has always been customer satisfaction. In our early days, we ran a small workshop where we supplied turned components to Escorts' tractor division. Because of our timely deliveries and quality work, Escorts started calling us "Turner Brothers." That name wasn't just a title—it was a reflection of our dedication to doing things the right way. We even received awards and appreciation from Escorts, which boosted our confidence and reputation.

Another pillar of our success has been the support of our family. I used to work alongside my elder brother in the factory, and it was because of his guidance and help that I was able to move forward. We all worked hard together, supported each other fully, and made sure we had each other's backs. That sense of togetherness has been the backbone of our success. We've lived and worked as a unit, and that unity has helped us overcome many challenges.

One thing I realized early on is that you can't grow if you stick to the same old ways of doing things. You have to be open to change and always ready to adapt. When I first started, we were just a job-work company. But in 1979, we decided to take a big step and started manufacturing material-handling equipment.

This shift wasn't just about expanding the business—it was about aligning our values with a clear strategy. We've always believed in delivering the best to customers, and that mindset helped us achieve some major milestones. Whether it was earning recognition from Escorts or becoming pioneers in our industry, everything we accomplished was because of this alignment between our values and our business goals.

Keep Learning: The Key to Growth

I believe that every interaction—whether with a helper, worker, manager, factory owner, friend, or family member—has something to offer. There's always a chance to learn something new, whether it's a piece of knowledge or a solution to a problem you've been stuck on for hours or even years. I've been lucky to have many chances to learn, both through formal training and informal experiences.

One of the best learning opportunities I had was when Escorts sent us for a 15-day training in Japan through AOTS. There, we listened to experienced Japanese teachers and business professionals who shared real-world tips and advice. We also visited several Japanese manufacturers, and I was amazed by their commitment to work, discipline, and excellence. We took many of their ideas and applied them to our own businesses.

Another great experience was a 15-day training in Rotterdam, Netherlands, through CBI under a World Bank project. This training helped us understand how important things like catalogs, presentations, marketing, and etiquette are in business. It also gave us the chance to attend exhibitions in Hannover at a very low cost. These two training experiences, combined with four international exhibitions, helped us grow in many ways and took us several steps ahead.

I also learned a lot from visiting factories in countries like Germany, Finland, the U.K., France, and Czechoslovakia. These visits were extremely valuable, and I made sure to apply whatever we could to improve our work. Even with limited financial resources, we always focused on improving our products, providing better services, and striving for excellence in everything we did.

I also have a big library of books and magazines in my room. The books range from engineering handbooks to soft skills and business management. I have a habit of going through trade magazines and exhibition materials and noting down new innovations or products that could somehow be used by us to improve the quality or efficiency of our work.

I always tell my team to ask questions. In today's world, where information is so readily available, we have actually stopped asking questions. People feel that by asking questions, they might be considered foolish. But that's not true—ask questions and keep the learning attitude alive. When we visited a big engineering company in Japan, the CEO of the company came from the accounts department. From my inquisitive mindset, I asked him, "How can you run an engineering company without a technical background?" He answered, "Just ask questions—relevant questions. Sometimes, being 'dumb' helps."

It was a big learning experience for me as well.

What I've learned from all these experiences is simple: *Keep learning, because the more you learn, the more you grow.* Every new piece of knowledge or skill helps you improve and take your business or life to the next level. Whether it's from people, places, or experiences, you never know when you'll find something that makes a big difference. So, never stop learning—it's the key to success.

Organized: The Art of Being Systematic

Staying organised helps you stay ahead. I have always been a well-organised person, much like one would expect from a corporate professional. Every interaction I have, I note down in my diary. There was a time when we found ourselves stuck in a case, and I was able to trace back a meeting summary from two years ago, simply by looking through my past diaries. It's amazing how being organised without technology can still lead to clarity and solutions.

Smile

A smile can break barriers and create an instant bond. One thing I hear time and again is how infectious my smile is. Whether it's in person or on the phone, I greet everyone with a smile, no matter what challenges I might be facing. No matter the situation, maintaining a positive attitude and a friendly demeanor can help you connect with people. It's not just about maintaining positivity; it's about making others feel at ease, encouraging them to open up, and helping them smile too. When you approach others with warmth, you create an environment of trust and collaboration.

Contacts

Your network is your net worth. I believe that relationships are the key to everything. I make it a point to remember and reconnect with every person I meet. Once a month, I scroll through my contacts or revisit visiting cards, randomly reaching out to check on people's well-being. This habit has been instrumental in solving problems. Whatever the issue, someone in my contact list always has the solution. A quick call and the matter is resolved in no time.

Open to All

In the corporate world, hierarchy is often strictly maintained, but that's not how I operate. My door is open to everyone—whether it's a peon or a senior vice president, all are treated with the same respect and enthusiasm. I prefer to spend less time in my cabin and more time with the people, sitting at their desks to understand their issues and find solutions together. It creates a sense of satisfaction and ownership in them, 'which is priceless.

Remembering Names

I strongly believe in the power of names. Whether it's a team member, worker, or client, I make it a point to remember their name. And I carry this belief into my practice, remembering the names of all the 400 individuals who work with us, as well as our clients. It's a small act, but it goes a long way in building strong, personal connections.

It shows that you see them as an individual, not just a face in the crowd.

Manifestation

Manifesting your goals and desires plays a powerful role in achieving success. I practice this daily through my morning prayers, where I give my challenges to God and ask for guidance. Once you focus on a goal with a strong desire, the universe aligns to help you find solutions. It's about trusting the process and knowing that everything will come together when you truly believe.

Forgiveness

Forgiveness is a beautiful practice that helps you let go of negativity. I've learned to forgive anyone who wrongs me, freeing myself from carrying any resentment. Letting go of grudges enables me to move forward with a clear mind and heart, making room for growth and positive energy in both my personal and professional life.

I believe that every human is a creation of God and that we are here to serve. A human can make mistakes, and forgiveness is an internal attribute for me. I don't know why, but I don't judge people based on their past deeds, which helps me a lot in return. There have been instances where people have wronged me, and the next time they meet me, I treat them as a new person, as if nothing had happened. This opens up many possibilities for me. Forgiving and considering past deeds as consequences of situations help me speak with positive energy every time. There is no prejudice in my mind, which always fosters positive discussions.

Never Procrastinate

One more important lesson I've learned is never to procrastinate. Whenever there's a task to be done or a call to be made, I do it immediately rather than delaying it. This simple but powerful lesson has taught me that when you get the thought or the urge to do something, you should act on it right away. If you wait or procrastinate, the task might never get done. Don't put off for later what you can do now.

Solve customer problems

Focus on solving problems is one of the major criterias for Reva rising so fast in the already crowded space. I remember sitting in L&T, and we were discussing a special requirement of theirs where the material was to be shifted horizontally instead of vertically. L&T engineer Mr. SM Rao discussed this with me and told me they had a budget of 50 lakhs for this. In those times, 50 lakhs used to be a huge amount. I told him a simple solution of having pulleys and a winch to solve this problem, which cost only 1.5 lakhs. Since then, Reva has been in the good books of

L&T. SM Rao used to praise us in every meet of L&T. So, focus on solving problems, not just earning money or ditching others.

Adopted Wisdom

I've always lived by the famous saying: "Life is not a matter of holding good cards, but of playing a poor hand well." This mindset has helped me tackle difficult situations with determination and skill. Another saying I follow closely is: "If you wait for all the lights to turn green, you'll never leave the driveway." We often wait for the perfect moment, but life doesn't always work that way. While proper planning and timing are important, sometimes you just need to jump in and go with the flow. The way forward will become clearer as you move ahead.

These values have shaped my journey, not just as a professional, but as someone who believes in people, organisation, and the power of connection. They've guided me through challenges and helped me build a business that thrives on mutual respect and efficiency.

By applying these values in your daily life and work, you'll notice a change in how you connect with people, solve problems, and grow your business. It's not just about success—it's about building strong relationships and creating a solid foundation for long-term growth.

CHAPTER 5

Fearless Vision and Revolutionary Change

In business, success doesn't come easily. It takes bold decisions, a clear vision, and the courage to do things differently. We have always believed that we possess these qualities, which have helped us throughout our journey. We weren't just running a business; we were building something for the future. I dared to think ahead of my time, and I was committed to changing the way things were done.

High Standards Since the 1980s: The Reva Way

Our clients expect high standards from us, and we are thankful to all those clients who continually raised the bar. Their expectations set off a chain reaction—prompting us to expect more from ourselves, which, in turn, inspired our team to hold themselves to even higher standards. It is these high client expectations that have shaped Reva into what it is today.

We look forward to client feedback because they are our consultants, guiding us on the path to improvement. I remember an incident in the late 1980s during a BHEL project, where the consultant rejected all the hoists we had manufactured due to the drum thickness being less than specified in the drawings. Although we had used plates of adequate thickness, the removal of ovality in the pipe led to a slight reduction in thickness at certain points. We replaced the drums entirely and learned a valuable lesson. Since then, we've ensured such complaints do not recur. We started using seamless pipes for drums (as ovality is not an issue) at that time, which no one else in the industry was using. Our suggestion and request to incorporate the use of seamless pipes were included in IS:3177 in 1999, and to this day, we continue to use seamless pipes for drums.

To this day, we conduct rigorous monthly meetings to address site issues and take immediate action to prevent repetition.

In India, it is common to hold back 5%-10% of the payment as a performance guarantee for cranes, which is paid after one year of successful commissioning or against a bank guarantee. Many crane manufacturers forfeit this 10% as their quality standards fail to meet customer expectations. For them, 90% customer satisfaction is acceptable. They may save a little money, but they ultimately cause inconvenience to the most important stakeholder—the customer.

At Reva, we ensure our cranes perform reliably even beyond the one-year guarantee period. In fact, we offer a 10-year warranty on our gearboxes—a commitment few others dare to match. This confidence stems from the quality of our products and our stringent manufacturing standards.

Our quality control team comprises approximately 10 members dedicated solely to this function, whereas our competitors, operating at a similar level, typically employ 20-30 staff in total, with only 2-3 dedicated to quality. At Reva, we have in-house facilities for UltraSonic Testing (UT), Magnetic Particle Testing

(MPI), Universal Testing Machine (UTM), Hardness Testing, Surface Roughness Testing, Hook Proof Load Testing, Vibration and Noise Testing, DFT (Dry Film Thickness), Megger Insulation Resistance Testing, and more. These resources ensure that strict quality checks are consistently upheld.

We also conduct annual maintenance training workshops, educating both customers and non-customers. This initiative stems from our desire to see India progress, as cranes play a crucial role in enhancing productivity across industries.

High standards must always be accompanied by humility. Arrogance is the death of high standards. At Reva, we are proud of our products, but we are never arrogant. I personally ensure I stay grounded by greeting every worker daily and praying to God to keep me humble. One can remain humble by doing small, small activities like I make up my bed every morning and night, keeping my soil plates in the washbasin, etc. These small activities keep the humbleness alive in you.

I firmly believe that culture flows from the top. My attitude influences my team, and it is my responsibility to cultivate a culture of respect, modesty, and customer-centric values. Maintaining humility ensures that, regardless of how excellent our products are or how knowledgeable we may be, there is always room for improvement and learning.

I strongly believe that achieving high standards requires a culture of humility and vulnerability. I encourage team members to embrace these values. We are human, and we all make mistakes. The first step toward improvement is acknowledging when we are wrong. Only then can we find ways to improve.

Expecting high standards from oneself drives innovation and continuous improvement. What is exceptional today will become average over time unless we push ourselves to do even better in the future.

Key Turning Points in Business

The first major turning point in our journey was shifting our work from Anand Parbat to Okhla Industrial Area. Another significant milestone was when Mr. M.M. Anand Ram, the ex-Chief Engineer of K.G. Khosla's Crane Division joined us. On my elder brother's advice, we started the Lifting Equipment Division. We began with manual chain pulleys and small manual cranes.

Such was the confidence that in 1981-82, I went to Mazgaon Docks to participate in a tender for a 25-ton chain pulley block. I had never known anything technical about it, except for a drawing and its understanding from Mr. Anand Ram. I was able to convince the CME at Mazgaon Docks, who accepted and placed an order for 12 units of 25-ton chain pulley blocks. We had never made a chain pulley block of this capacity earlier, but the confidence arises within based on your team and self performances.

Being associated with original equipment manufacturers like Escorts, Eicher, and the Vehicle Factory taught us the importance of correct materials and manufacturing processes and quality products.

We benchmarked a well-known European crane manufacturer and tried to incorporate their designs, manufacturing processes, and testing methods to improve the quality and acceptability of our products—all while keeping the equipment affordable.

We achieved several firsts in the industry and **I was also awarded the Udyog Patra in 1986 by the then Vice President of India, Dr. Shankar Dayal Sharma. and Test of Fire by Haryana Chief Minister Shri Bhupender Singh Hooda**.

- First Manufacturer in India to Obtain the ISI Mark on Chain Pulley Blocks
- First in the Country to Obtain ISO-9001 Certification
- In 1998, First Indian Participant at the Hannover Trade Fair for EOT Cranes and Electric Hoists, a move that helped us assess where we stood technologically against global players.

Pioneering Technology in an Era of Hesitation (1990)

Back in 1990, the business world in India was very different. At that time, computers were not seen as something necessary for running a business. In fact, they were considered luxuries, far removed from the daily operations of factories or companies. Most companies, particularly in industries like cranes and hoists, relied on manual processes and didn't see the need for change.

But we didn't follow the crowd. We believed in the power of technology, even when others didn't. We made the bold decision to introduce computers in our company—not just for accounting, but for every single part of our operations. This was completely new at the time.

To make this vision a reality, we sought out the best talent available. We hired engineers from IIT to develop software specifically for designing cranes, replacing the old manual calculations and paper blueprints. At the same time, we gathered a team to create an in-house ERP system, which was another first for us. This was not just about adopting new technology—it was about leading our industry into the future. Under my leadership, our company, Reva, became a modern, tech-driven operation, setting new standards that others started to follow.

Keep the Prices Competitive: Our major success was due to being extremely cautious about pricing. In the 1990s, there were big players like Mukund and Jessop who dominated the railway's crane requirements. We disrupted the market with our competitive prices and high-quality products.

This was only possible because we focused on keeping expenses low. At the same time, we made sure our products were top-notch. We kept improving our processes, came up with new ideas, and learned from our mistakes along the way.

Customer Focus: Don't focus on what competitors are doing; instead, concentrate on what the customer wants. By continuously prioritizing customer requirements, we have grown to where we are today.

I remember the early days when I didn't even know the meaning of QAP (Quality Assurance Plan). Reva is a product of listening to customer demands and implementing their suggestions. Even today, I make it a point to meet visiting inspectors, interact with them, and learn how we can improve. I firmly believe there is always room for improvement.

To this day, we follow strict component identification and traceability for every part used in Reva cranes. This process, taught to us by NTPC in the 1990s, involves using GE number procedures to ensure traceability, guaranteeing quality and reliability.

Many competitors have copied our designs, poached our team members, and even replicated our crane design software. However, I am not worried because I firmly believe that while external aspects can be imitated, my soul cannot. They might create better designs by building upon ours, but the internal spirit of customer care is something they can never replicate.

Interestingly, some of the people who were poached by competitors, even at double the salary, could not sustain the environment. This is because the competitors' primary goal was to copy and understand Reva's workings, not to genuinely care about their people or customers.

Reva is built on the foundation of customer focus. This focus is evident in everything we do. Employees may come and go, but this foundation remains unshaken.

Taking Reva Global: The Australian Exhibition (1993)

By 1993, even before the technological advancements, I had already started thinking globally for Reva. While most Indian crane companies were focusing only on the Indian market, we decided to take a bold step: to participate in an international exhibition in Australia.

It wasn't an easy decision to make. It required a lot of resources, careful planning, and, most importantly, belief in ourselves and our product. Back then, it was rare for a company from India to showcase its products in a global exhibition. But we had full faith in the quality of our work and believed that we could make an impact beyond India too.

The Australian exhibition was a milestone—it was a huge turning point not just for Reva but for the entire Indian crane industry. It showed that Indian companies could compete on the global stage and succeed.

However, during the exhibition, something unexpected and striking caught my attention. As I observed the various products on display, I noticed that our hoist, which had a 2-ton capacity, appeared significantly bulkier compared to the sleek and compact designs of the other hoists from around the world. It wasn't just my observation—visitors to our stall would often ask, "Is this a second-hand hoist, or is it a 10-ton hoist?" The questions were not just a passing curiosity; they felt like a direct challenge to the hard work we had put into creating the product. I couldn't help but feel insulted. It was as if all the effort we had invested in the design and development of the hoist had been overlooked in favor of its outward appearance. I stood there, almost frozen, for much of the day at the exhibition, unable to shake off the feeling of discouragement.

But this experience, while disheartening, became a pivotal moment for us—a challenge that we decided to take on head-on. We couldn't allow our product to be judged solely by its size and external features. We were determined to not only improve the efficiency and functionality of our hoists but also to make them more compact, visually appealing, and aligned with global standards. The path forward was clear: we had to innovate. To make our hoists more competitive, we chose to incorporate advanced materials, such as low-carbon alloy steels for the gears and pinions. This would improve the strength and durability of the components while reducing the overall weight. Alongside this, we focused on optimizing the design to ensure that it was more streamlined and in line with the best practices in the industry. Our goal was to transform our hoists into a product that would not only stand out for its performance but also for its modern, efficient design.

At the same time, we realized that VVVF Drives weren't readily available in India. So, we decided to consult with IIT Delhi and take the bold step of developing our own VVVF Drive. While it only remained a prototype, it was a big step forward for us and showed that we were willing to take on any challenge to improve our products and serve our customers better.

At the time, all the capital goods required for railway workshops were being procured from a central organization. This organization was also responsible for studying new technologies and revising their specifications to keep up with advancements. I had the opportunity to visit their library. There, I found hundreds of technical literatures from world-class manufacturers, along with numerous technical books. I spent countless hours coordinating the insights from these literatures with the technical books, gaining a deeper understanding of global best practices.

Some forward-thinking senior engineers, holding CME rank, took my observations seriously. They recognized the importance of keeping the interests of all manufacturers in mind and took the initiative to redraft the crane specifications in line with global practices. They ensured that the new specifications were accessible to all manufacturers with only a minimal effort required for adoption, while also ensuring that the latest technologies remained affordable. This was a huge milestone in our industry's growth.

I even succeeded in convincing the Bureau of Indian Standards to incorporate these changes into national standards, making it easier for all manufacturers to adopt them. This was a game-changer, helping to elevate the Indian crane industry to a global level.

My Take on This

These key moments in our journey are a reflection of how we've approached business:

- We didn't just follow trends; we created them.
- We weren't afraid to take risks, even when the stakes were high.
- We combined vision with hard work, ensuring that every bold idea was executed with determination.

Through these fearless decisions and my unwavering commitment to innovation, we didn't just build a successful business—we paved a path that inspired others to dream bigger and reach for more. Our approach showed that it was possible to break free from the conventional norms and make a meaningful impact in their respective fields..

CHAPTER 6

Resilience in Adversity – The True Test of Leadership

In business, having a clear vision and fearlessness is key for any leader, but what truly shapes their legacy is their resilience and commitment to doing things the right way. My journey hasn't been easy. There were many tough moments, but it was during these challenging times that my true character came to the forefront. Adversity tested me in every way possible, but my strength, courage, and strong values helped me not just survive but thrive, and I've always tried to inspire others to keep going, no matter what.

A Leap of Faith: The CNC Machine Revolution (1996)

By 1996, most of the crane industry was still using traditional methods of manufacturing. But I could see that the future was in automation and precision. I knew that by investing in advanced CNC (Computer Numerical Control) machines, we could improve our manufacturing and gain a competitive edge.

But we didn't stop at just buying one or two machines. I had a vision of transforming our entire production process. So, I traveled to Germany, a hub of industrial technology, and purchased six high-quality second-hand CNC machines. Once the machines arrived in India, setting them up and getting them integrated into our process wasn't easy. It took long hours of hard work, but it was worth it. This wasn't just an investment in machinery; it was an investment in the future of our company.

While others in the industry were hesitant to even consider automation, we went ahead with it, and that decision set Reva apart.

Adopting Global Standards: ISO 9001 (1998)

In 1998, long before it became a common practice for Indian companies, we made the bold decision to pursue ISO 9001 certification for Reva. At the time, many questioned why we needed an international standard, but we saw it as an invaluable opportunity to enhance the efficiency of our processes and, most importantly, to demonstrate our commitment to quality on a global scale. This wasn't just about acquiring a certificate; it was about building credibility and showcasing to our customers—both in India and abroad—that we stood firmly for excellence in everything we did.

Our efforts didn't go unnoticed. Not only did we successfully achieve the certification, but we were also recognized for our commitment to quality and awarded with cash prizes as a testament to our dedication. This was a significant milestone in our journey, reinforcing our position as leaders in the industry.

Pro-Engineer 3D Solid Modeling Software with FEM Analysis: Bringing Design to Life in 3D (2000)

By the year 2000, the design industry had started using 3D modeling, but most companies in India were still stuck with old methods. We recognized the potential of 3D to change the way cranes were designed. We decided to introduce this cutting-edge software to Reva, making us one of the first in the crane industry to use 3D modeling. This move helped us stay ahead of the curve and strengthened our reputation as an innovative company.

Global Outreach: Exhibitions in Germany, England, and India

Taking Reva to international exhibitions wasn't just about showcasing our products; it was about putting India on the global map for the crane industry. In the 1990s and early 2000s, many Indian companies were focused solely on the domestic market, but we knew that we had the potential to make an impact globally. Germany and England were countries known for their industrial expertise, and exhibiting there was a bold step. It allowed us to learn from the best, network with global players, and prove that Indian companies could hold their own on the world stage. These exhibitions helped us expand our horizons and put us in a position to compete globally.

In the same year, I had a strong urge to do things differently. As the saying goes, "When everyone is doing ZIG, you should ZAG. And when they are doing ZAG, you should do ZIG." This mindset has always pushed me to think outside the box.

While older technologies weren't necessarily bad, they often resulted in bulkier and heavier cranes. After comparing technical data, we realized that we could have saved around 28% in materials if we had applied the techniques used in today's cranes. The cranes we built then are still working as good as new. In fact, just recently, we received a message from a company that shared a picture of a crane we made back in 1986. And it was still working perfectly. That made me very happy.

Overcoming Adversity and Embracing Failures

Strength and resilience in the face of failure have been constant companions in my journey. There were times when we faced worker strikes, and I had to navigate through those challenges. Reva was shut down due to disputes in 2003, and those two years were undoubtedly the most difficult of my life. But I held on to my belief that God helps those who help themselves. I remained focused and determined to get out of that situation. And with time, we emerged stronger and more committed to our goals.

Speaking of adversity and embarrassing situations, I recall an incident, as mentioned earlier, when our factory was closed due to internal disputes, and bank operations were also halted. This created a severe cash flow issue, and we couldn't pay the provident fund to the department, which led to constant follow-ups. One day, I received news that the authorities were planning to arrest me. I tried to avoid the situation, but one morning, officers from the PF office arrived at our residence. I had just started my morning prayers when my wife informed me that some people were looking for me. In a panic, I ran to the rooftop of our neighbor's house, and my family told the officers that I had left early in the morning. They warned us, saying they would take strict action unless I reported to their office immediately.

By God's grace, I was able to arrange a senior officer's recommendation. I went to the PF office, explained my difficulties, and asked for time, but they were firm. They told me that I was under arrest and would not be allowed to leave. However, with the senior officer's intervention, the PF authorities agreed to give me two months to resolve the matter, and I was released.

This experience taught me the importance of staying calm in the face of pressure and relying on my faith and resilience to navigate through even the most difficult situations.

CHAPTER 7

Rising Through the Storm

In 2003, things went wrong within the family, and internal disputes led to the temporary closure of Reva. This was one of the toughest times in our company's history. The factory doors were shut, creditors were angry, and we were facing trouble from everywhere—banks, the excise department, sales tax officials, and even labor unions. It seemed like everything was falling apart. But no matter the circumstances, I never allowed myself to break. I kept my phone on, because I knew running away wasn't an option. I faced the creditors with humility and patience, enduring hours of questioning by excise officers. There was even an incident when a labor union leader physically attacked me, snapping my neck in the process. Despite everything, I stood tall because I knew that my courage wasn't just for the company—it was for the future of my family.

During this period of closure, I advised my son to start a new company called "Reva Cranes and Hoists." At least this way, we could continue serving our loyal clients while the main business was on hold. I made it clear to him—Reva's products were my creation, my "baby," and I couldn't let them be lost. So, we started the business in a small room, focusing on repairs and maintenance for our existing cranes.

What surprised me the most was the support we received from our workers. They joined us without hesitation, and not once did they ask for on-time salaries. They were just happy to serve, and they believed in the company's mission. I remember how our senior fitter would sometimes pay the workers' salaries from his own account, saying, "Sir, whatever I have earned, it's because of you." It's moments like these that made me realize how deep-rooted our values were in the company.

Starting the business in that small room was one thing, but the real challenge was getting finances to keep it running. There were nights when we didn't even have enough money to buy food. But this is where relationships came into play. My friends and family stepped forward to help. They offered generous amounts of money to help start the business. One of our machine dealers even provided us with four machines for free, saying, "Pay me when you can." Looking back, I see the value of relationships and how important it is to treat people with love and respect. In the journey of life, it's crucial to be helpful, treat people with love, and always respect them. They are all God's creatures, and we must respect them just as much as we love ourselves.

Serving the Customer – Our Top Priority

I have always believed that customer service should be our top priority. I often tell my son, "Do your work in such a way that the customer never has to worry." I say to him, "Cranes are like roofs of a building—no one wants a leak in their roof, and similarly, no one wants a crane that stops working. A crane should never stop—not even for a day. The work must go on." With this philosophy guiding me, I never paid much attention to what competitors were doing or how they managed to offer cranes at lower prices. My focus has always been on delivering unmatched quality.

We made sure that the components in our cranes were top-notch. The parts had to be made with the best machines, the designs had to use the latest software, and the workers had to get the best training. We were the first in the crane industry to introduce things like VVVF Drives, energy chains, low-carbon alloy steel, and CNC machines in North India. We didn't just follow trends—we set them.

Purpose in Life

There have been many times when my son asked me how I handle everything. "How do you stay involved in every small detail of the business without getting tired? How do you listen to angry clients and still manage to turn them into friends? This isn't the age to work so hard, Papa. You've already achieved so much—why do you still push yourself so much?"

I always reply, "Beta, God has given me the responsibility to take care of 400 families. That's where I get my energy from. My goal is to make it 800. The customer is the one who provides us with the money that supports our team. If the customer isn't happy, it means we aren't fulfilling our responsibility."

Sometimes, I tell my son that upon my death, he should be able to tell people, "He was fine, went to the factory, worked the whole day, and in the evening had a drink, took his dinner, and slept while talking to us. Unfortunately, he did not wake up the next morning."

I also tell him, "I want to die while working." To this, he replies, "Your dedication is unmatched, Papa. Hats off to you!"

Even now, I do something simple yet deeply meaningful every day. Before eating, I lift my plate slightly, thank God, and say, "Rab 2 roti sab nu dein" (May God give two meals to everyone). It's my way of reminding myself that no matter how much we achieve, gratitude and humility should always come first.

Gratitude is present in every word I speak. I thank God every moment, and I am deeply grateful for the people around me—my team, my family, and everyone who makes this world so beautiful.

CHAPTER 8

A Fresh Start: The Revival of Reva

After a three-year hiatus, we decided to give Reva a fresh start, driven by a renewed sense of purpose. The decision wasn't easy, but when I took that first step, to my surprise, the customers welcomed the reformed company with open arms. Over the years, I had worked hard to build trust, integrity, and a reputation based on honesty and ethical conduct. Now, it was time for those values to pay off.

The name Reva had developed such strength and goodwill that it wasn't just a restart; it was a revival. It became a testament to my belief in the principle:

"Kar Bhala to ho Bhala."

(Do good, and good will come to you.)

I am a strong believer in this quote and have witnessed it many times in my life. There have been many instances when our bank limits were exhausted, and we had to pay our vendors as per the payment terms. My accounts person would come and ask, "Sir, what should we do? Should we delay the payments?" I would tell him to prepare the cheques, and the universe will listen to our intentions. In all cases, the payment from clients was received within a maximum of 2 days from the date of preparing our cheques.

If your true intention is to pay, then the universe will listen, and a way will be found. Because of this, Reva is recognized as a good paymaster. We have intentionally not delayed anyone's payment to date, whether it be our vendors, partners, or employees. This also reflects why we are in business. We are in business to serve 400 families currently, and we are in business to help clients reduce their material handling worries by making cranes with 99% uptime.

YES Attitude

I firmly believe in the power of saying "YES." I feel that starting with a "NO" might mean rejecting an opportunity that God has planned for you. Anything you approach with a "NO" energy results in less-than-100% effort, ultimately leading to an unfinished task. Every individual possesses unique skills, and the universe has a way of presenting challenges tailored to one's capabilities. So, accept the challenge and always begin with a "YES."

Never be discouraged by failures. Keep trying, trying, and trying, and you will surely find a way. I always tell my team, "If it's not impossible, let's try to achieve something." This attitude has helped me a lot.

I can recall many instances where the "YES" attitude has helped me, but the road was never smooth always. When we restarted Reva, no bank was willing to offer us a credit limit because we had defaulted in the past. I approached several banks with our business plan, the required collateral, and documentation, but all of them denied our request. Some banks didn't even entertain us and outright refused to engage. The banks initially refused to offer us loans due to our past on the defaulters' list. Despite the rejections, I didn't lose hope and didn't let this setback break me.

This journey took almost a year. I knocked on every door, sought advice from my contacts, and eventually, Punjab National Bank agreed to finance us—though the interest rate was high. This is how Reva got its second chance. From that point on, there was no looking back.

Restoring Dignity: Repaying Debts and Winning Trust

Once the storm finally settled, we knew that we had a bigger responsibility to uphold—integrity. Despite the immense financial strain we were under, we made sure to repay every creditor, big or small, in full. But we didn't stop at paying off the debts; I personally wrote a thank-you note to each one, acknowledging their patience and support during those tough times.

This wasn't just a financial gesture; it was about rebuilding trust and restoring dignity. It was our way of showing that Reva stood by its word. Customers, employees, and suppliers saw this integrity in action, and it became the foundation upon which we rebuilt the company.

Innovation in Blood: Setting Standards for the Industry

At Reva, we have always believed that when the conversation turns to innovation in the crane industry, the first name that should come up is Reva. We made sure that, since our revival, this belief became a reality. ***Aur wo din tha, aur aaj ka din hai—hum aaj bhi yahi maan ke chalte hain.*** (That was the day, and even today, we walk with that same belief.)

Just recently, my son Rohit had a meeting with a senior person from Tata Steel. During this conversation, the senior official presented Rohit with a priceless gift—*the Reva Catalogue from the 1980s.*

He remarked that the entire crane industry was shocked by that catalogue. People were amazed at how Reva had the foresight to standardize and catalogue cranes in such a manner. This moment was a testament to our long-standing commitment to innovation—setting new standards even when the world was not ready for them.

World-Class Infrastructure: Building Excellence, Day by Day

But we didn't stop there. Innovation isn't just in ideas; it's in execution, and we continued to improve our infrastructure continuously. We built it day by day, not just to meet industry standards but to set them.

There was a time when Reva became so renowned that even NTPC (National Thermal Power Corporation) would refer to us as the go-to solution provider. Whether it was for quality checks or any other crane-related solution, Reva was the name everyone trusted. We weren't just a business; we became an institution within the industry.

Our commitment to excellence made us a name to reckon with, and our infrastructure stood as a symbol of the world-class standards we upheld. From the beginning of our revival to where we stand today, *Reva has always been a beacon of innovation, quality, and trust.*

Broad Vision

Having a broad vision for the future helps make routine problems seem small and easily manageable. It often leads to making the right decisions in the long term. I live by this principle, always considering future aspects and impacts while making decisions.

As narrated earlier, in 2008, we received a big order for a 100T crane. However, manufacturing such a crane was not possible in our existing premises. While renting a workplace could have been an easy solution, we chose to buy a factory space instead, seeing it as a signal from the universe. Although we were not financially strong at the time, we decided to invest in a 1.25-acre factory. My son and team members questioned this decision, asking, "What will we do with this huge space?" and "How will we manage the repayments?" Today, this factory is also too small for our needs. Back then, we built the factory with the vision of manufacturing cranes with capacities of up to 250T, and we successfully manufactured one in 2023. This experience reinforced the importance of having a future-focused vision, as the smaller concerns of repayment and similar challenges were easily overcome.

A similar situation arose in 2014 when we purchased land for a new factory at IMT Faridabad. It was a smaller piece of land intended for either renting out or manufacturing small parts. HSIDC initially allocated us a plot in a narrow street. However, I envisioned that if we started manufacturing cranes in this unit, transporting them through the narrow street would be difficult. With this in mind, I approached the HSIDC department and requested a change. They were kind enough to reallocate a plot with ample space in front, making transportation easier. Today, we manufacture cranes in this unit as well.

This journey demonstrates how having a broad vision can guide decisions and help tackle challenges effectively.

Abundance Over Scarcity

We don't believe in transactions; we believe in solving customer problems. Clients usually ask me to reduce the prices, which we don't agree to. I don't want to get into a scarcity mindset. If I get less, I would try to cut corners and save pennies, which would diminish the quality that Reva is known for. We believe in abundance, not scarcity, and we wish to give our customers more than what is expected of us, each and every time. I strongly believe that with good intentions, abundance can be obtained. Without good intentions, abundance will vanish.

There have been instances where our estimation made mistakes in quotations. In one case, we even made the mistake of quoting for 1 crane instead of 2 and got the order for 2 cranes at the price of 1. We honored our commitment and supplied the cranes. When abundance is present, good intentions are followed, and vice versa. We have a policy to hide the PO prices once the order is received because we don't want employees to distinguish between clients based on the prices. The quality should not be dependent on the price.

Playing the discount game cannot be a viable strategy. There are new crane fabricators coming up every month who rely solely on lower prices. Price wars only diminish the quality of the product and push us into a scarcity mindset. Work with integrity and honesty to solve customer problems, and you will find a place in the market.

Lessons from Adversity

These tough times taught me some invaluable lessons:

- **Resilience** isn't just about survival; it's about standing strong even when chaos surrounds you.
- **Integrity** builds bridges that no amount of wealth can.
- **Leading with courage and kindness** inspires trust and loyalty, even in the most challenging situations.

Through the hardships and the recovery, I realized that leadership isn't just about building a business—it's about building a legacy. A legacy rooted in values, trust, resilience, and a commitment to setting new standards of excellence.

❍ ❍ ❍ ❍

CHAPTER 9

Personal Growth and Challenges

Be Positive and Action-Oriented in Everything You Do

People often ask me, "How do you get results so easily? How can you turn difficult situations to your favor so effortlessly?"

I tell them: Deal with people as a friend, understand their needs, and approach them with genuine love and a true intention to help.

There have been countless incidents where a positive attitude, a willingness to serve, and asking for help with humility have yielded incredible results.

The Nursery Admission Experience

I still remember the day of my son Rohit's nursery admission interview at Apeejay School. It was a reputed institution, and we had heard that the principal was very strict. We were informed that the parents, along with the child, would also be interviewed.

My wife, Sunita, worked tirelessly with Rohit, teaching him poems and alphabets to prepare for the big day. When the interview day arrived, the principal began asking Rohit questions, followed by some pointed ones for us.

During the interaction, I treated the principal with warmth and respect, addressing her like a sister. I even invited her and her husband for dinner at our home, which she gracefully accepted. This dinner marked the beginning of a long-standing relationship. Years later, even in her last days, she helped secure my grandson's admission.

Finding a Home in Faridabad

In 2005, we were looking for a rented house in Faridabad. At that time, we had a big house in Delhi, but since Reva was closed and finances were tight, we had to move to a smaller, more budget-friendly house.

We saw many properties, but nothing came close to the lifestyle we were used to. Out of frustration, the dealer showed us a high-end property called "Royal Retreat" in Charmwood, Faridabad. My wife hesitated at the gate, saying, "This looks too expensive; we shouldn't waste our time."

But I insisted we take a look. The house was magnificent – massive rooms, huge balconies, 100% power backup – truly no less than a haveli. The dealer mentioned the starting rent was ₹1 lakh per month, which was way out of our budget.

Still, I decided to dig deeper and got the details of the landlord. To my surprise, they happened to be neighbors of my brother-in-law. They trusted us and graciously agreed to a rent of ₹25,000 per month. They were looking for reliable and responsible tenants, and we were a perfect match.

This experience taught me: Don't give up. Take a step forward, and you will find a way.

Delivering Under Pressure for BHEL

Two years ago, we were working on a critical project: manufacturing four 140-ton cranes for BHEL. The delivery timeline was tight because BHEL had delayed placing the order, and their client was under political pressure to deliver on time.

BHEL engineers often sat in my office for hours, expressing their concerns and pressuring us with their words, which could easily drive anyone crazy. Instead of getting overwhelmed, we understood their problems and reassured them repeatedly that we would meet the agreed schedule.

I committed a delivery date and, despite numerous challenges, our team worked tirelessly to honor it. That date happened to fall on a Sunday, but the crane inspection was completed as promised.

As a reward for our dedication, BHEL PEM ED honored me as the "Guest of Honour" at their vendor meet. I was invited to light the lamp in front of prominent companies like Kirloskar, L&T, and others. It was a proud and memorable achievement for me.

Remember: A positive attitude, coupled with genuine efforts, can turn even the toughest situations in your favor.

CHAPTER 10

Reflections and Learnings

In this chapter, I will share some of the key reflections and learnings that have shaped my journey. These realizations, drawn from my experiences, have played a pivotal role in how I approach both personal and professional challenges. I hope these learnings offer you valuable perspectives that can inspire and guide you in your own endeavors.

Follow Your Gut

Once, a journalist came to interview me and discussed the various attributes with which I operate. The first thing I told him was to follow your gut. I rely a lot on my gut feeling. If something feels right to me, I take quick action to implement it—whether it's employee selection, machine selection, or any other decision. In tough situations involving high risks, the most I do is ask God in my morning prayers, "What decision should I take? How should I resolve this particular situation?" The answer is always given by God. I consider that decision as God's decision and make sure that after taking it, I turn it into the right one. I strongly believe that gut feelings are decisions made by God, and we must follow them.

I also feel that when you are customer-focused, have integrity, and do not wish to harm anyone intentionally, the decisions you make are often correct.

Invest Back in the Business

One of the major reasons for our success is that we didn't take the money back home. Reva was treated as a separate entity, and whatever profits we earned were reinvested back into the company. This is one of the major mistakes made by entrepreneurs today. My father used to say, "With a factory, you can have many houses, but with a house, you cannot have enough factories." This is why we never invested in personal properties, and each year we would add more machines to build Reva stronger.

For years, our savings account used to have a zero balance. I still remember once when we were in the USA for a material handling exhibition. While returning, at the airport, Rohit wanted to buy a video camera. However, the debit card was declined because it didn't have enough money.

Give Your 100% Each Time

Every time you do anything, ask yourself: Are you giving 100% of yourself? I remember the days when we used to stay awake all night preparing for tenders the next day. I remember the nights when workers stayed up, working tirelessly to honor our customers' requirements. I am grateful to my team, both past and present, who have worked relentlessly, giving their 100% each and every time.

Giving 100% in everything you do is essential. In the early 1990s, I started going to the gym and doing aerobics. I gave it my all and went from 90kg to 67kg—a breakthrough in my health. I trained myself so well that, on days when the aerobics instructor was absent, I was selected to conduct the classes.

The way you do anything is the way you do everything. If you want to check whether you're giving 100%, start by examining how you do the small things, as they are easier to identify. This will help you correct your path.

Once, Warren Buffet was asked to participate in a $5 bet with his friends. Each friend would contribute $5, and if the golf ball went into the hole in one strike, he would win $1,000. Warren Buffet declined, saying that the probability of winning was less than 1%, and he didn't want to be part of such a bet. His friends urged him, saying it was only $5 and not to spoil the fun. But he refused. This is why Warren Buffet is at the level he is today. The way you do anything is the way you do everything.

Challenge yourself every day to learn something new, to do better than yesterday. Train your body and mind to face challenges. It could be as small as going to the gym every day and doing a bit more than yesterday. Train your body and mind to do extra, and you will be able to apply this in every aspect of your life. I sincerely feel that the rituals of our forefathers, like fasting, were based on this principle—to challenge your body and mind apart from having health benefits. I, to this date, keep fast during Navratras twice a year. I pray to God every morning to give me the strength to better support my people and clients and to give me new ideas to perform better.

Employee Training

Reva is also known as a learning temple. The seniors are always in constant endeavor to help the juniors learn. There are weekly training schedules, both from internal and external sources, creating a growth-oriented environment.

Our team often says, "What I learned in other companies in three years, my colleagues have learned here in three months."

As a result, people from Reva are often poached with double the salary offers. However, they return due to the love and the environment we strive to maintain.

Culture Matters

We only hire people who align with our culture. We have a culture of integrity, humility, authenticity, vulnerability, and continuous learning and teaching. Those who don't match our culture leave us soon, while those who do often return, even after spending years with other companies.

We hire people who value service and are committed to improving themselves day by day. Both of these attributes require a learning and training mindset. We teach service by emphasizing training, and this culture of service is enhanced to deliver a better crane each time.

I always tell new joiners that we are a close-knit family. For us, words matter more than papers. I believe employment is like marriage—it's meant to last. Marriage requires trust to function, and being authentic and honest is one of the most important attributes sought after. The foundation of trust is honesty, and if trust is broken, the marriage will not survive.

If a person is not strong enough to acknowledge their mistakes, misguides others, blames others, or makes excuses, they cannot improve or grow. People like this are parted from the team.

We have team members who joined us in the early 1990s, and they still visit me to meet and seek guidance. I am open to all and always wish them the best in their careers and lives.

Employees Are Not Made to Work Till Exhaustion

We do expect high standards and 100% effort from the team every single time; however, we ensure that our team is not mentally fatigued to the point of burnout. We strongly believe in maintaining a balance between high productivity and well-being. We know that when our employees are physically and mentally at their best, they can achieve far more than when overworked and exhausted.

To encourage this, we used to have a monthly enjoyment party at my house, where all senior and mid-level team members would join for drinks and dinner, enjoying the evening with singing, dancing, and laughter together. These gatherings were more than just a celebration; they were an opportunity to build strong relationships and bond outside of work.

Additionally, all the seniors used to have lunch together in my room, and a potluck was organized where each day a senior member would bring lunch for everyone. It was a time to relax, exchange ideas, and discuss both our successes and challenges in a casual setting. This informal atmosphere helped create an open, collaborative environment. We would chit-chat, discuss wins and failures, and enjoy lunch together, which brought everyone closer as a team.

Over the years, several annual trips were organized each year, where all Reva members visited sacred places like Naina Devi, Haridwar, and other religious sites. These trips were not only spiritually enriching but also created lasting memories and a deeper sense of connection within the team. The team bonding reached a whole new level as we shared experiences, celebrated each other's growth, and created a strong sense of unity that carried over into our work.

Think Differently

I am very passionate about doing things differently. From something as small as traveling on less-traveled roads, like if I have to go to Chandigarh from Faridabad, the usual route is via Delhi. However, I prefer going through the newly developed expressway. It might be a longer route, but my passion for doing things differently helps me achieve what others are afraid of, while they remain in the rat race, following what everyone else is doing.

Whether it's buying a car, purchasing a machine, or even normal routine work, I tend to think differently. It's not always that my decisions are correct, but making decisions is important. This ability of mine helps me find out-of-the-box solutions and not just follow the crowd.

Everett Rogers' Diffusion of Innovations Theory states that only 2.5% are innovators and 13% are early adopters. I consider myself an early adopter—I am open to new ideas and implement them quickly.

Travel Like a King

I always believe that when you are traveling for work to other cities and towns, you should keep comfort in mind. As owners of SMEs, we have a tendency to save money, but I believe that you should stay in a good hotel so you can sleep well and be active when meeting clients. I remember once traveling to Chennai and staying in a 5-star hotel. I even wrote a postcard to my wife, Sunita, saying that the tea here costs 150 rupees. It's not that comfort consumed me—I have also traveled many times by train, sitting by the side of the toilet on the floor when tickets weren't reserved. But, generally speaking, travel should be comfortable. The goal is to remain fresh and attentive for client visits.

CHAPTER 11

More Than Just Business

In this chapter, I want to share what my loved ones—my daughter, son, granddaughter, and wife—have to say about me. They've always been there, supporting me every step of the way. While my experiences in business have played a big role in shaping my career, it's the lessons, values, and love from my family that have truly shaped the person I am today. Their voices reflect the emotional side of this journey, offering insights into how my actions and beliefs have impacted them.

My Wife Sunita Goel:

Balraj Ji is an emotional man, and one moment that stays with me is during our Vidai, when he saw me crying, he couldn't hold back his own tears. Despite life's challenges, his positive thinking and ability to solve problems have always driven him forward. His guidance to Rohit, our son, during his early years and his involvement in Rohit's journey has played a key role in shaping the person he is today. Together, they have helped bring our family to the successful place we are now.

My Daughter Pooja Goel:

One of the most meaningful things I remember from my childhood is how Papa would always lift his plate slightly before eating, thank God, and say, "Rab 2 roti sab nu dein"—"May God give two meals to everyone." At first, it seemed like just a small habit, but as I've gotten older, I've realized how much it has impacted me. It taught me the importance of gratitude and kindness in the simplest, most powerful way. This small act has shaped how I see the world, and I carry it with me every day.

Papa's larger-than-life presence was always evident. I remember hearing our grandfather call him a "babbar sher" (lion)—a term that perfectly describes his courage and determination. It's something I've always admired about him, his strength and willpower to keep moving forward, no matter what. His sense of humor, too, added so much joy to our lives. Papa would sit us down and make us laugh with his many styles of laughter, always lifting our spirits.

My Son Rohit Goel:

Papa has always had a passion for music, particularly Pankaj Udhas's ghazals. I still remember how he would insist I record his favorite song, "Hothon Se Chulo Tum," on a cassette for him, so it could play on repeat in his car. Music parties at our home, where clients and team members came together, were a regular affair. These gatherings were more than just work; they were about building relationships and creating an environment of warmth and camaraderie.

Papa's ability to network and connect with people, whether in business or personal life, is something I've learned from him. He made it effortless, a skill I truly admire. I remember how he impressed even the strictest admission teachers, ensuring that I had the opportunity to join the best school. This is just one example of how he turned challenges into opportunities with his charm and networking skills.

My Grand-Daughter Sayesha Goel:

I learned a valuable lesson from Dadu during my search for an internship. When I was feeling lost and frustrated, he shared something that stuck with me: "Everything comes to those who hustle while they wait." His words pushed me to keep working hard and following up, even when I wasn't sure what would happen next. This advice has stayed with me and continues to help me face every challenge that comes my way.

Dadu's lessons aren't just about business. He taught me to value our cultural and religious traditions, showing me the importance of reflecting on and learning from texts like the Bhagavad Gita and Hanuman Chalisa. When I was in 6th grade, he arranged for me to take tuition classes to learn the Sunder Kand from the Ramayana. His way of living, based on gratitude, has influenced how I see the world. Even though he's older now, Dadu still goes to the office every day because he understands the impact his work has on the lives of many people. His sense of responsibility towards others is something I try to live by every day.

Dadu, we want to dedicate you something...

A Man of Many Roles

A father, a guide, a steady hand,
The one who taught us how to stand.
With wisdom deep and heart so wide,
In his love, we always abide.

A husband true, a partner strong,
Through life's dance, he leads along.
With every smile, with every care,
A bond so pure, beyond compare.

A brother's strength, a shoulder firm,
Through every trial, he stands unturned.
Sharing laughter, easing pain,
In his presence, joy remains.

A grandfather's warmth, a gentle embrace,
Lighting young hearts with his grace.
Telling tales of times gone by,
A living legacy, our reason why.

In every role, he gives his all,
A towering figure, yet humble and small.
The thread that binds, the rock we trust,
A life so noble, so kind, so just.

This book is a tribute, a heartfelt song,
To the man who's been our anchor all along.
A life of love, a life well-spent,
A life that inspires, a life heaven-sent.

Thank You For Always Being There!!!

Gratitude as a Way of Life

Gratitude is not only about saying words to express thanks to God; it goes beyond that. It's an act of kindness and about giving back to society. I am grateful to the people I meet, grateful to God for giving me such a wonderful life, and for the people around me who give me strength. Throughout the day, during my prayers, both consciously and subconsciously, I thank the Universe for everything I have been given. It's my favorite saying: "Bhagwan ka lakh lakh shukriya. I never imagined that I would be receiving this much. It's all the blessings of the elders and God that they have given me such a beautiful life."

Whenever something positive happens, my first response is to thank GOD for the blessings, and then we celebrate by distributing ladoos to every employee. This small celebration now happens only when the order value exceeds One Crore. It's a gesture of sharing and making everyone feel involved in the day-to-day work, reminding us all that we are part of something bigger.

I give bajra and roti to the birds early in the morning as an act of gratitude to the Universe for such a wonderful environment, where the birds chirp and the lush greenery surrounds me. As part of my routine, I also give some cash to the sweepers in the morning—just a small token of gratitude for the work they do in maintaining cleanliness around us. These simple acts remind me that nothing is too small when it comes to giving back. Gratitude isn't just about the grand gestures; it is about the small, consistent acts that make a difference in the world around us.

I offer a roti to the cow every day in the morning, as my parents taught me that cows are like mothers. Touching and patting the cow's head brings me internal pleasure and satisfaction. It reminds me of the simple joys in life and the value of nurturing the world around us.

Personally, I am an extremely satisfied person and thank GOD at every step for the life he has given me. Especially when I reflect on the fact that I am an ordinary person with no fancy education, no business background, and very limited intelligence, I feel truly blessed. Whenever an employee comes to me, I try to offer the maximum help I can, whether it's related to a medical issue or a family event like a marriage. I always strive to provide whatever assistance I can. The more we give, the more we receive in unexpected and fulfilling ways.

The End is Just the Beginning

Everything comes to those who hustle while they wait.

So, we've come to the end of this chapter, but it's really just the beginning of the journey we're on together. Over the past 56 years, I've learned so much, and in this book, I've shared the lessons and experiences that I believe can help you on your own path to success. It's not just about what I've done—it's about what you can take from this to make your own journey better.

I truly hope this book helps you, just as my experiences have shaped my life. If you have any questions, thoughts, or just want to discuss anything in the book, I'm here for you. I'd love to hear what you think, and I'm always happy to help with anything you need.

Feel free to reach out to me. Your feedback means a lot, and I'm excited to hear from you!

Email Id: cmd@revacranes.com